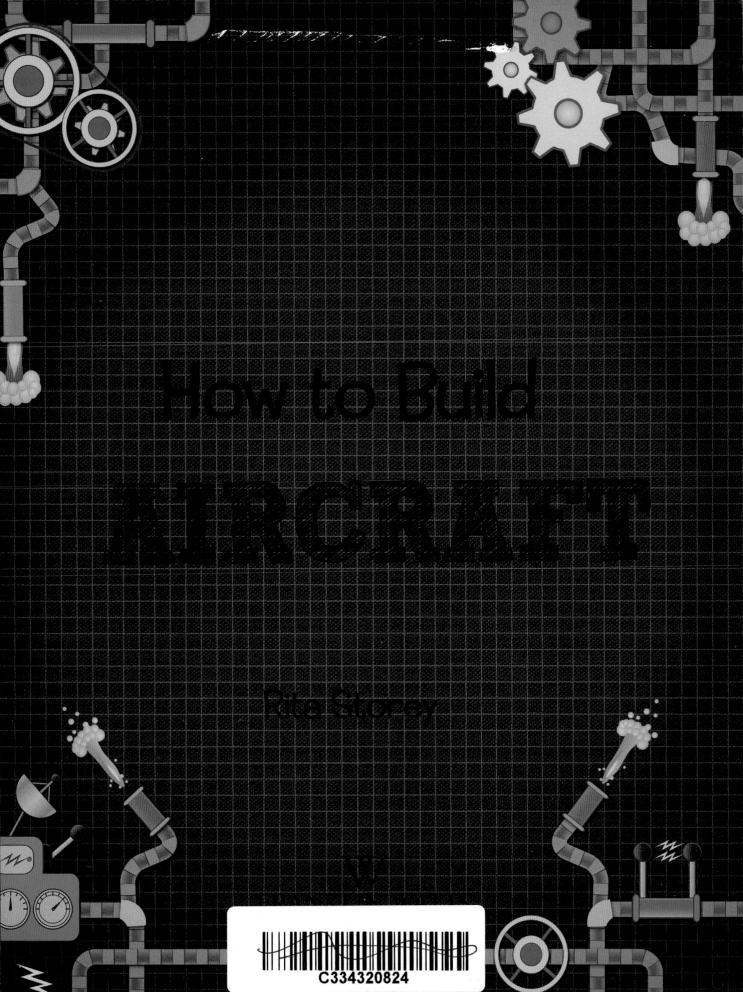

How to Build

AIRCRAFT

Rita Storey

C334320824

Franklin Watts
Published in Great Britain in 2018 by
The Watts Publishing Group

Copyright © The Watts Publishing Group, 2016

All rights reserved.

Credits
Executive Editor: Adrian Cole
Packaged by: Storeybooks
Design Manager: Peter Scoulding
Cover design and illustrations: Cathryn Gilbert

Dewey number 629.2'22
ISBN 978 1 4451 4471 9

Printed in China

MIX
Paper from
responsible sources
FSC® C104740

FSC
www.fsc.org

Picture credits
The publishers would like to thank the following for permission to reproduce their
pictures: Billyhill: (middle right), Chowells: 4 (bottom), Cpl Andy Benson/RAF; Cpl
Lee Goddard/RAF: p5 (middle left); Juan Lacruz: 4 (top); Library of Congress: (middle
right); Mike Peel: 4 (middle); Mike Young at English Wikipedia; (top right); Mitruch:
4 (middle); ReptOn1x: 15 (bottom); Trev M: (bottom left); US Air Force (middle right,
bottom right); US Oceanic and Atmospheric Administration (bottom right);
Step-by-step photography by Tudor Photography, Banbury.

Every attempt has been made to clear copyright. Should there be any inadvertent
omission please apply to the publisher for rectification.

Franklin Watts
An imprint of
Hachette Children's Group
Part of The Watts Publishing Group
Carmelite House
50 Victoria Embankment
London EC4Y 0DZ

An Hachette UK Company
www.hachette.co.uk

www.franklinwatts.co.uk

CONTENTS

SAFETY FIRS

Some of the projects
book require scissors,
tools or a hot glue gun.
using these things we
recommend that chil
are supervised by
responsible adult

Flying machines

Have you ever wondered how people learnt to build flying machines?

For centuries people tried to copy the way birds fly, fixing man-made wings to their bodies and flapping them. This was very unsuccessful and eventually engineers found other ways of getting airborne.

Gliding and floating

Gliders, paragliders and hang-gliders are flying machines that bring humans as close as they can get to bird flight. These machines have no power source, so they glide through the air silently, riding on currents of air.

They stay up in the air because air moves faster over the top of their angled wings than beneath them, causing higher pressure that results in lift. With no engine to generate thrust, these flying machines have to start their journey from a high place or be towed into the air and launched.

Hot-air balloons float up because the hot air trapped inside them is lighter than the colder air surrounding them.

Powered flight

Adding an engine and a propeller to a winged flying machine allows it to generate thrust and take off into the air under its own power. Add a jet engine to an aeroplane and you are really going places. Engineers design aeroplanes to suit their intended use. The Spitfire's wing shape (left) and powerful engine gave RAF pilots a plane with the ability to make tight turns during the Second World War (1939 – 1945).

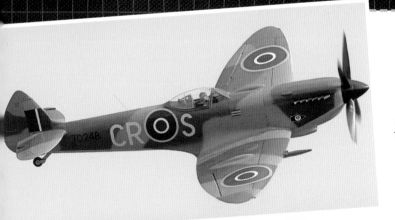

Civil aviation

Every day, all around the world, aeroplanes transport passengers and cargo over short distances and long ones. Air traffic controllers track the movement of planes that are in the air, guiding pilots safely through busy international airspace. These planes vary in size from the eight-seater Britten-Norman Islander, designed for short hops between islands, to the monster Airbus A380, which can carry up to 853 passengers on international flights.

Aircraft at war

The demands of war have boosted the development of aircraft design from the earliest days. Some aircraft, including Chinook helicopters (left), are used to carry troops and equipment while others, such as B-2 Spirit (below), are designed to fly undetected on spying missions. In battle, fast fighter planes are used for air-to-air combat, and bomber aircraft carry bombs or missiles.

Drones

Unmanned Aerial Vehicles (UAVs), usually known as drones, are controlled remotely by a crew on the ground. These pilotless vehicles are used for gathering information as well as for dropping bombs.

The US Predator (right) was the first military drone. It could fly for as long as 40 hours at altitudes of up to 7,600 m on reconnaissance or deadly bombing missions.

Engineers are always searching for new ways to design aircraft. The Boeing X-51A Waverider (left) has travelled at hypersonic speeds of Mach 5 (almost 6,430 kph) In test flights.

Before you get started on each of the projects in this book, you'll need to gather together the materials and tools listed in the 'you will need' box. Hopefully you will have most things to hand, but some of the more unusual items can be bought from suppliers listed on page 32.

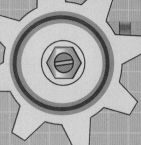
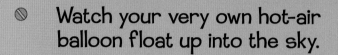

Hot-air balloon

Watch your very own hot-air balloon float up into the sky.

Why does this happen? The hot air inside the balloon is lighter than the cold air all around it. When the air inside the balloon cools down, it will sink back down to the ground.

To make the hot-air balloon you will need:
- 2 x large, thin bin bags
- sticky tape
- paper or plastic cup • scissors
- ruler
- 4 x 30 cm lengths of string

1

Cut the bottom off one bin bag so that it forms a tube. Tape it to the open end of the second bin bag. Make sure there are no gaps where air could escape when the bin-bag balloon is being filled with hot air.

2

Tie four knots in the open end.

3

5CM

Cut the bottom 5 cm off the paper cup. Carefully use the point of the scissors to make four holes equally spaced around the edge of the paper cup.

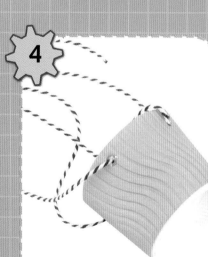

4

Tie one end of each length of string through the holes in the paper cup.

5

Tie the other end of each string onto a knot on the bin-bag balloon.

To launch the hot-air balloon you will need:
- hairdryer
- access to a plug socket
- paper and pen to record what happens

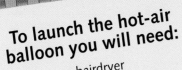

SAFETY FIRST

This hot-air balloon is uncontrollable. It will be carried by the wind. It is best to fly the balloon in a space with a high ceiling, such as a school hall, but you could launch it outdoors on a day without wind. If you do, keep it away from roads and power lines. Pick up the hot-air balloon when it has landed.

6

Put the nozzle of the hairdryer through the opening at the bottom of the bin-bag balloon. Turn the hairdryer on and wait until the balloon is full of hot air. Watch your hot-air balloon float up into the air!

A fair test
Try making these adjustments to the hot-air balloon. Make one change at a time.

- What happens if you make a bigger balloon?
- How far does the balloon travel if you place a toy passenger in the paper cup basket?
- What happens if you use a different type of bin bag?

Aircraft science

To design aircraft you need to understand the four forces that will act on them as they fly. In an ideal design, all four forces are evenly balanced.

Lift is the force that keeps an aeroplane in the air. The plane's wings form a special shape called an aerofoil that generates a pushing force from below the wings, called lift. For more on this, read about Bernoulli's Principle at the bottom of this page.

Drag is the force of resistance that tries to stop an aeroplane from moving through the air. Friction causes drag. Good aeroplane design minimises drag.

Thrust is the forward movement of an aeroplane. This can be generated by a rocket engine or by rotating propeller blades powered by the plane's engines.

Gravity is the force that pulls an aeroplane down towards Earth. Lightweight materials will help fight against the pull of gravity.

Aerodynamics

How easily an aeroplane moves through the air is called its aerodynamics. It is an important factor in aeroplane design.

Bernoulli's Principle

Engineers use Bernoulli's Principle, named after Swiss mathematician Daniel Bernoulli, to design aircraft. The principle explains the relationship between aircraft wing shape and the pushing force, lift.

Most aircraft wings are rounded at the top and flatter at the bottom, forming an aerofoil. As the aircraft moves forward, its wings push through the air. The air moving over the top of the wings moves a little faster than the air travelling underneath the wings, creating lower air pressure on top of the wings and higher air pressure beneath the wings. This pushes the aircraft up into the air – a force called lift.

FASTER MOVING AIR

aerofoil

SLOWER MOVING AIR

LIFT

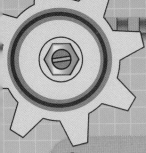

Roto-copter

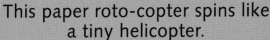

This paper roto-copter spins like a tiny helicopter.

Why does it spin? As the roto-copter falls, air pushes up against the rotor blades, bending them slightly. As the blades bend, some of the upwards thrust becomes a sideways push. Since the 'push' from each blade pushes in the opposite direction, this makes the roto-copter spin, rather than move sideways.

To make the roto-copter you will need:
- sheet of paper, 18 cm x 9 cm
- pencil
- ruler
- scissors
- paper clip

1

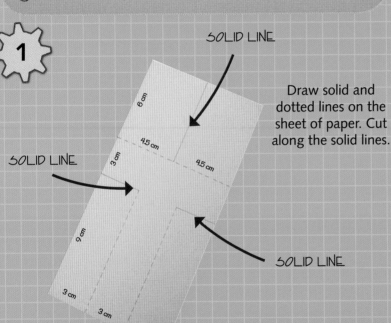

SOLID LINE

SOLID LINE

SOLID LINE

6 cm

4.5 cm

3 cm

4.5 cm

9 cm

3 cm

3 cm

3 cm

Draw solid and dotted lines on the sheet of paper. Cut along the solid lines.

2

Fold the top right strip down along the dotted line. Crease along the fold.

3

Turn the paper over. Fold the top right strip down level with the fold of the first strip. Crease along the fold.

4

Open out the folds at the top. Fold along the two vertical dotted lines, folding the paper into the middle to form a stem.

5

Fold up 1 cm of the paper stem at the base of the roto-copter. Slide the paper clip on.

STEM

Try this!

Open out the paper and use crayons or felt-tip pens to decorate the roto-copter. Fold it back into shape.
What happens to the colours when the roto-copter spins?

SAFETY FIRST

Ask an adult to supervise when you launch your roto-copter. Do not lean out of the window, and take care if you are standing on steps. Stretch your arm out to drop the roto-copter away from your body.

To launch the roto-copter you will need:

• something solid to stand on, such as a pair of steps or a staircase OR you can launch the roto-copter from a first-floor window
• paper and pen to record your findings

6

Hold the roto-copter away from your body by the stem above the paper clip and throw it into the air. Watch it spin to the ground!

A fair test
Try making these adjustments to the roto-copter. Only change one thing at a time and record what happens.
• How does it affect the flight if you make a bigger roto-copter?
• What happens if you change the length of the roto-copter blades?
• What happens if you use a heavier paper clip?
• Does it make a difference if you use thicker paper?

10

Whirligig

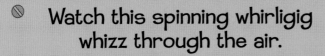

Watch this spinning whirligig whizz through the air.

How does it work? As the whirligig falls, air pushes up against its blades but also pushes sideways on them. This makes the whirligig spin around and move sideways through the air.

To make the whirligig you will need:
- wooden craft stick
- dish containing warm water
- paint and paintbrush
- hot glue gun
- pencil

1

2 Hold both ends of the stick between your finger and thumb. Gently twist one end towards you and the other end away from you until the craft stick stays twisted when you let go. Leave to dry.

SAFETY FIRST
Ask an adult to supervise when you use the hot glue gun.

Put the craft stick into a dish of warm water. Leave it for an hour.

3

Paint the craft stick. Leave to dry.

Use the hot glue gun to put a blob of glue on the end of the pencil. Place it in the centre of the craft stick. Hold it in place until it cools (this will only take a few seconds).

4

With your hands pressed together, hold the pencil between the fingers of your right hand and the palm of your left hand. Very quickly pull back your left hand and push forward your right hand. The whirligig will shoot off, spinning as it goes.

The hammer glider

Turn a sheet of paper into an awesome flying machine.

How does the hammer glider fly? When you throw the glider into the air, the force you use creates thrust. The force that keeps it in the air is called lift. To find out about lift and thrust, see page 8.

To make the hammer glider you will need:
- A4 sheet of thin paper
- ruler
- decorative craft tape
- scissors

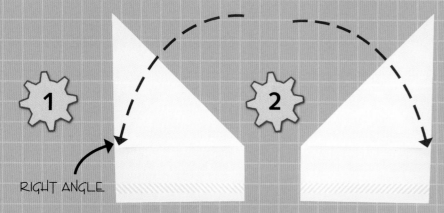

1 RIGHT ANGLE

Stick a piece of craft tape 1 cm from the bottom of the sheet of paper. Trim the ends. Turn the paper over. Repeat on the other side. Fold the right-hand corner down at a right angle. Crease and unfold.

2

Fold the left-hand corner down at a right angle. Crease and unfold.

3 CREASE

Fold the top right corner down so that the long edge rests along the diagonal crease.

4

Fold the top left corner down so that the long edge rests along the other diagonal crease.

5

Fold the paper in half. Crease and unfold.

6

Fold the top down to the bottom edge. Match up the edges.

7 Fold the right side of the folded paper to where the crease lines form a cross. Crease along the fold.

8 Fold the left side of the folded paper in the same way. Crease along the fold.

9 Open out the folds you made in steps 7 and 8.

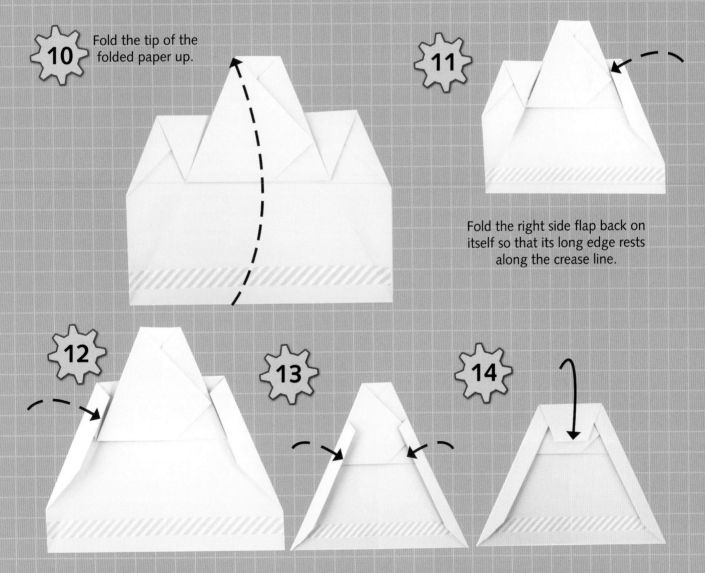

10 Fold the tip of the folded paper up.

11 Fold the right side flap back on itself so that its long edge rests along the crease line.

12 Fold the left side flap in the same way.

13 Fold both sides over once more, along the crease lines.

14 Fold the top down.

FOLD

Fold both sides together along the crease that runs along the length of what will be the glider's body, with the flaps on the outside.

Fold one wing down so that its edge meets up with the central fold.

Turn over. Fold the second wing down so that its edge meets up with the central fold. Open out the glider.

SAFETY FIRST

Even simple paper gliders can be dangerous. Find an open space where you are in no danger of hitting anyone. Aim the glider at a specific point.

To launch the hammer glider you will need:

- an open space

NOSE

18 Hold the glider gently, with your finger and thumb either side of the central fold. Pull back your hand and launch the glider into the air in front of you, with the nose pointing slightly upwards.

How to fly a plane

Flying a plane

A pilot uses cockpit controls to move parts of the plane in order to change direction.

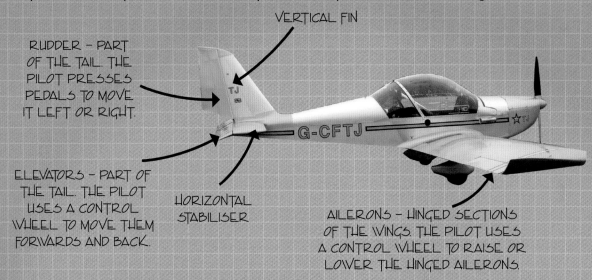

VERTICAL FIN

RUDDER – PART OF THE TAIL. THE PILOT PRESSES PEDALS TO MOVE IT LEFT OR RIGHT.

ELEVATORS – PART OF THE TAIL. THE PILOT USES A CONTROL WHEEL TO MOVE THEM FORWARDS AND BACK.

HORIZONTAL STABILISER

G-CFTJ

AILERONS – HINGED SECTIONS OF THE WINGS. THE PILOT USES A CONTROL WHEEL TO RAISE OR LOWER THE HINGED AILERONS.

To fly an aircraft straight and level a pilot controls three types of movement on three axis.

Pitch: rotation around the side-to-side axis. The pilot raises or lowers the elevators on the tail piece to control pitch. By controlling the pitch of the plane, the pilot makes the plane descend or ascend.

Yaw: rotation around the vertical axis. The pilot moves the rudder to the left or the right to control the yaw. By moving the rudder and the ailerons, the pilot turns the plane.

VERTICAL AXIS

HORIZONTAL AXIS

SIDE-TO-SIDE AXIS

Roll: rotation around the horizontal axis. By raising or lowering the ailerons on the wings, the pilot makes the plane roll to the left or right, which helps to turn the plane.

To see animations of these movements visit:
www.grc.nasa.gov/www/k-12/airplane/roll.html
www.grc.nasa.gov/www/k-12/airplane/yaw.html
www.grc.nasa.gov/www/k-12/airplane/pitch.html

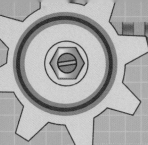

Bernoulli glider

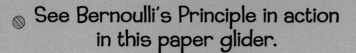

See Bernoulli's Principle in action in this paper glider.

This glider's wings form an aerofoil. The air moving over the curved upper shape travels a little faster than the air travelling underneath the flatter underside. This creates lower air pressure above the wings and higher air pressure beneath the wings, leading to lift, which pushes the glider up into the air.

To make a Bernoulli glider you will need:
- pencil and thin white paper (for tracing the template)
- A4 sheet of thick wrapping paper
- scissors
- double-sided tape

1

Use the pencil and thin white paper to trace the template on page 29. Cut it out and draw around it on the wrapping paper.

2

Cut out the paper glider shape.

3

FOLD AND CREASE

Fold the glider shape in half lengthways. Crease and unfold.

4

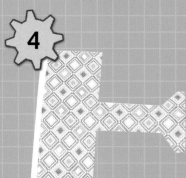

Stick a thin strip of double-sided tape along the front edge. Peel off the backing paper.

5

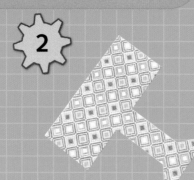

X

X

Fold the front edge back on itself but DO NOT crease along the fold. Press the two edges together between the points marked X, sticking them together along the length of the double-sided tape.

6

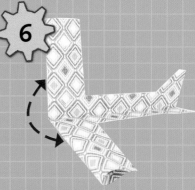

Fold the glider in half along its length. Open it out, keeping a semi-folded shape.

To launch the Bernoulli glider you will need:
- an open space
- paper and pen to record what happens

SAFETY FIRST
Even simple paper gliders can be dangerous. Find an open space where you are in no danger of hitting anyone.
Aim the glider at a specific point.

7 Hold the glider lightly underneath, between your thumb and finger. Launch the glider into the air in front of you with the nose pointing slightly upwards.

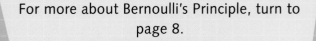

A fair test
Try making these adjustments to the Bernoulli glider. Only change one thing at a time and record what happens.
- What happens if you add a small blob of sticky tack to the nose of the glider?
- How does the glider fly if you make four cuts in the tail and fold the tail up to form two flaps?

For more about Bernoulli's Principle, turn to page 8.

If you make adjustments to the way the glider flies (see 'A fair test' left), you will see the effects that a pilot can make on an aeroplane's flight by using some of the cockpit controls (see page 15 for more on this).

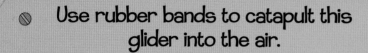

Catapult glider

Use rubber bands to catapult this glider into the air.

How does this work? The glider is made from light materials that make it stay airborne. It is launched into the air with the thrust from the energy stored in the rubber bands.

To make the catapult glider you will need:

- pencil and thin white paper (for tracing the template)
- A4 sheet thick paper
- scissors
- straight drinking straw
- 2 x 6-cm long rubber bands
- stapler

1

Trace the template on page 28 and use it to cut out one wing and two tail pieces from the thick paper.

2

Fold the wing piece along the centre, unfold it and place it on top of the drinking straw. Loop the rubber band under the drinking straw at the back of the wing.

3

Pull the free loop of the rubber band over the paper wing and loop it around the drinking straw at the other side of the wing.

4

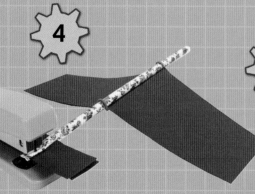

Turn it over and use the scissors to make a horizontal cut in the end of the drinking straw. Slide in the tail pieces. Staple them in place. Turn it over. Bend the wings up around the drinking straw.

5

Fold the top tail piece up around the drinking straw.

6

Push the end of the second rubber band into the end of the drinking straw at the nose of the glider. Staple it in place.

To launch the catapult glider you will need:

- a lolly stick (ask an adult to cut a small notch out of one end)
- paper and pen to record what happens

SAFETY FIRST
This paper glider can travel at high speed. Find an open space where you are in no danger of hitting anyone. Aim the glider at a specific point.

7 Hook the elastic band at the front of the glider into the notch in the lolly stick. Hold the glider between the wing and the tail. Point the glider's nose up into the air.

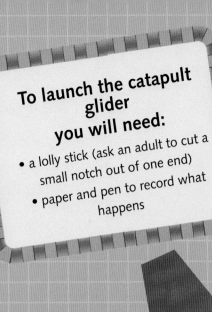

8 Pull back on the glider. Let go and watch it catapult into the air!

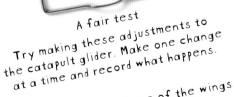

A fair test
Try making these adjustments to the catapult glider. Make one change at a time and record what happens.

- Try changing the shape of the wings.
- What happens if you slide the wings backwards?
- What happens if you slide the wings forwards?
- Try using thinner paper.

Glitch Fix!
Glitch: the glider nose dives.
Fix: find the centre of gravity by placing the drinking straw part of the glider on your fingertip. Slide the wings backwards or forwards until the glider balances.

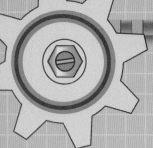

Rubber-band helicopter

⊘ **Create a working helicopter using** ⊘
a propeller and a rubber band.

How does it work? Energy is stored in the rubber band by winding the propeller. When the helicopter is launched, the rubber band releases energy, which turns the propeller. As the propeller spins it pushes air behind it, which pulls the helicopter forward.

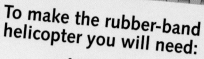

To make the rubber-band helicopter you will need:

- paper clip
- 18-cm blade, hook nose propeller (available from hobby shops)
- balsa wood stick, 4 mm x 6 mm x 15 cm
- sticky tape
- pencil and thin white paper (for tracing the template)
- 7-cm long elastic band
- thin card
- glue and spreader

1

Slide the propeller onto the end of the balsa wood stick.

2

Bend the paper clip.

3

Place it on the other end of the balsa wood stick.

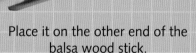

4

Use sticky tape to attach the paper clip where it touches the balsa wood stick.

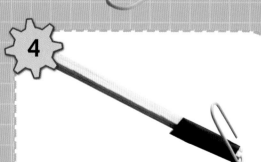

5

Loop one end of the rubber band onto the hook under the propeller.

HOOK

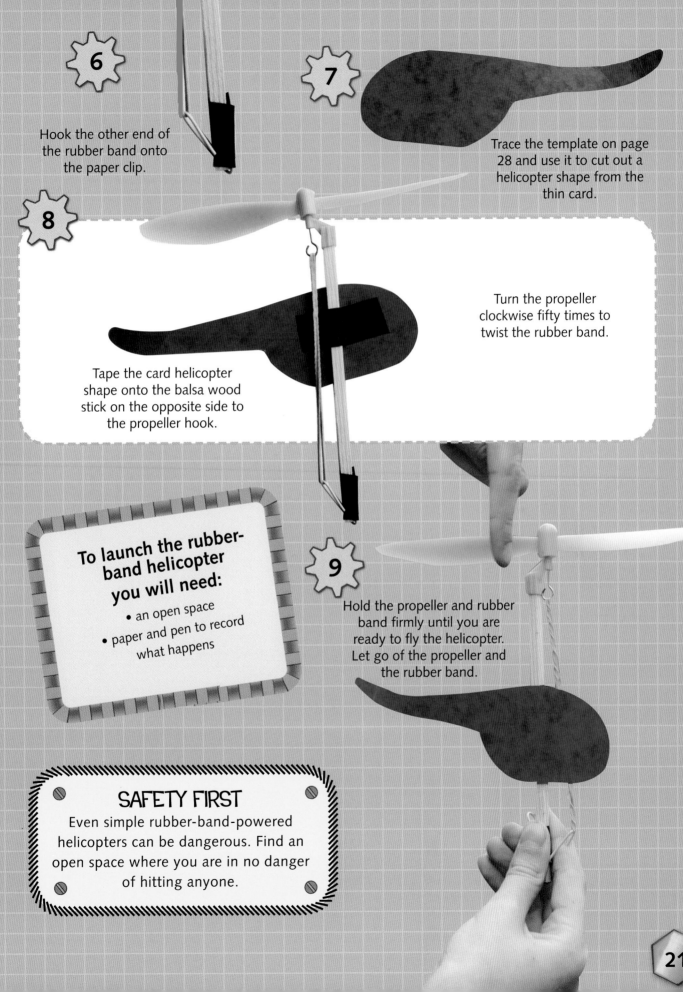

6

Hook the other end of the rubber band onto the paper clip.

7

Trace the template on page 28 and use it to cut out a helicopter shape from the thin card.

8

Tape the card helicopter shape onto the balsa wood stick on the opposite side to the propeller hook.

Turn the propeller clockwise fifty times to twist the rubber band.

To launch the rubber-band helicopter you will need:
- an open space
- paper and pen to record what happens

9

Hold the propeller and rubber band firmly until you are ready to fly the helicopter. Let go of the propeller and the rubber band.

SAFETY FIRST
Even simple rubber-band-powered helicopters can be dangerous. Find an open space where you are in no danger of hitting anyone.

Rubber-band plane

Made carefully, this plane can soar high into the sky.

How does it work? Energy is stored in the rubber band by winding the propeller. When you let go of the propeller, the rubber band releases its stored energy, which turns the propeller. As the propeller spins, it pushes air backwards and the aeroplane flies forwards. The light materials used to make this plane help it stay in the air and defy gravity.

To make the rubber-band plane you will need:
- balsa wood stick, 6.4 mm x 6.4 mm x 35 mm (or the same size as the hole in the propeller)
- 15-cm blade, hook nose propeller (available from hobby shops)
- 30-cm length of rubber band
- paper clip
- pliers • ruler
- pencil and 2 x sheets of thin white paper (for tracing the templates)
- A3 sheet of tissue paper
- masking tape
- glue stick
- packet of balsa wood strips, 5 mm x 3.5 mm x 30 mm
- hot glue gun
- felt-tip pen
- 4 x cocktail sticks
- scissors

1

Push the balsa wood stick into the propeller.

2

Place the ends of the rubber band together and tie them in a knot. Slide the knot along the rubber band to the end to create a big loop.

3

SAFETY FIRST
Ask an adult to supervise when you use the pliers.

Open out the paper clip.
Use pliers to cut off 2.5 cm on one end and bend the other end.

4

SAFETY FIRST
Ask an adult to supervise when you use the hot glue gun.

Loop the rubber band over the hook that is part of the propeller. Pull on the knotted end of the rubber band until the band is straight but not over stretched. Make a pencil mark on the balsa wood, just by the knot.

Push the straight end of the paper clip into the balsa wood where you made the mark. Use the hot glue gun to fix it in place, with the bent part angled away from the propeller. Leave it to dry. Loop over the knotted end of the rubber band. Set to one side.

6

stabiliser

rudder

Use the thin white paper to trace the templates on page 29. Cut a piece of tissue paper and use masking tape to tape it in place on top of the traced templates.

OPEN SIDE

7

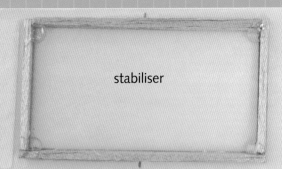

stabiliser

rudder

Use scissors to cut four pieces of balsa wood that will fit along the edges of the stabiliser piece. Glue the balsa wood strips onto the tissue paper using the glue stick. Make sure the corners touch. Use a blob of hot glue to join the corners. Leave to set.

Use scissors to cut three balsa wood pieces to fit the top, right side and bottom edges of the rudder section. Glue the balsa wood strips onto the tissue paper using the glue stick. Make sure the corners touch. Use a blob of hot glue to join the corners. Leave to set.

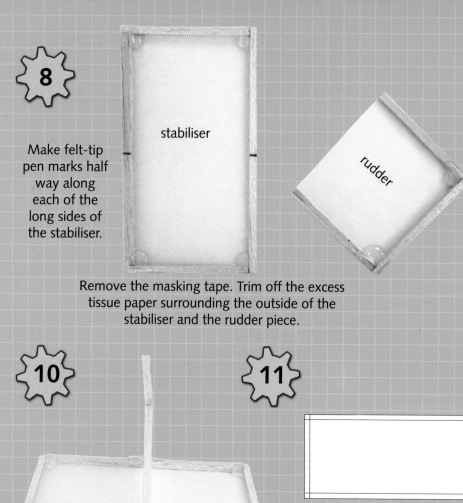

8

Make felt-tip pen marks half way along each of the long sides of the stabiliser.

stabiliser

rudder

9

Use the hot glue gun to stick the ends of the wooden strips of the rudder to the stabiliser. Leave to set.

Remove the masking tape. Trim off the excess tissue paper surrounding the outside of the stabiliser and the rudder piece.

10

The rudder must be at a 90 degree angle to the stabiliser. This is the tail piece of the plane.

11

FOLD

Follow the instructions on page 29 to trace and cut out the wings. Unfold.

12

Tape a sheet of tissue paper over the traced template.

13

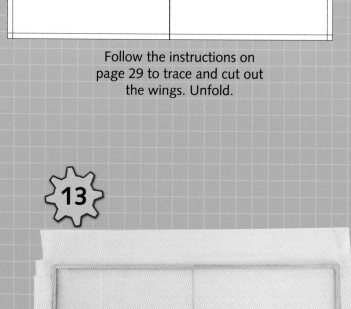

Cut strips of balsa wood to fit around the edges of the wing piece.

14

Use the glue stick to fix the balsa wood strips onto the tissue paper. Make sure that the ends touch at the corners.

15

Use a blob of hot glue on each corner. Leave to dry.

16

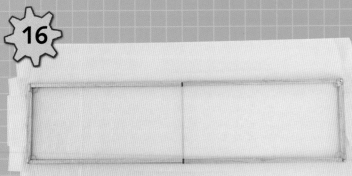

Use a felt-tip pen to mark the balsa wood at the centre of the long sides of the wing piece.

17

Remove the masking tape. Trim away the excess tissue paper.

18

10 CM LENGTH OF BALSA WOOD

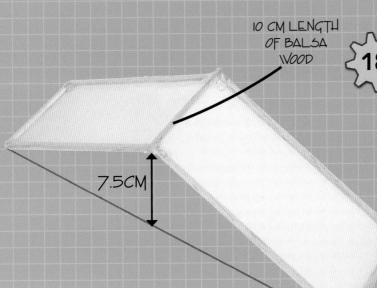

7.5CM

With the balsa wood strips on the outside, carefully bend the wings at the halfway marks. Prop the wing piece up on a table so that the highest point is 7.5 cm above the table. Stick a 10 cm length of balsa wood across the centre of the wing using the hot glue gun. It will overhang a bit on each side.

Use scissors to cut the sharp points off the cocktail sticks.

Use the hot glue gun to stick a cocktail stick to each side of the central strip of balsa wood. Leave to dry.

With the elastic band under the balsa wood body of the plane (the fuselage), use the hot glue gun to attach the tail piece you completed in step 10. Only glue the balsa wood, not the tissue paper. Leave to dry.

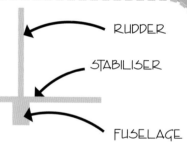

RUDDER

STABILISER

FUSELAGE

The rudder and stabiliser should be in line with the end of the fuselage.

Use the hot glue gun to stick two of the cocktail sticks that form part of the wing piece either side of the fuselage, about 7.5 cm from the propeller.

Now glue the other cocktail sticks on the wing section so that they end 1 cm below the fuselage. This means that the wings will be angled, aiding flight.

To launch the rubber-band plane you will need:

- plenty of space • a stopwatch (and a friend to use it)
- paper and pen to record what happens

23

Wind the propeller clockwise fifty times to twist the rubber band.

24

Hold the plane up in the air. Ask a friend to be ready to press the stopwatch the moment you launch the plane and stop it when the plane lands. Let go of the propeller and watch the test flight. Record the length of the flight.

A fair test

Try making these adjustments to the rubber-band plane. Make one change at a time and record what happens.

- What happens if you make more turns on the rubber band?
- What happens if you try to wind the propeller the other way?

Templates

Rubber-band helicopter, pages 20-21

Catapult glider, pages 18-19

Cut 1

Catapult glider, pages 18-19

Cut 2

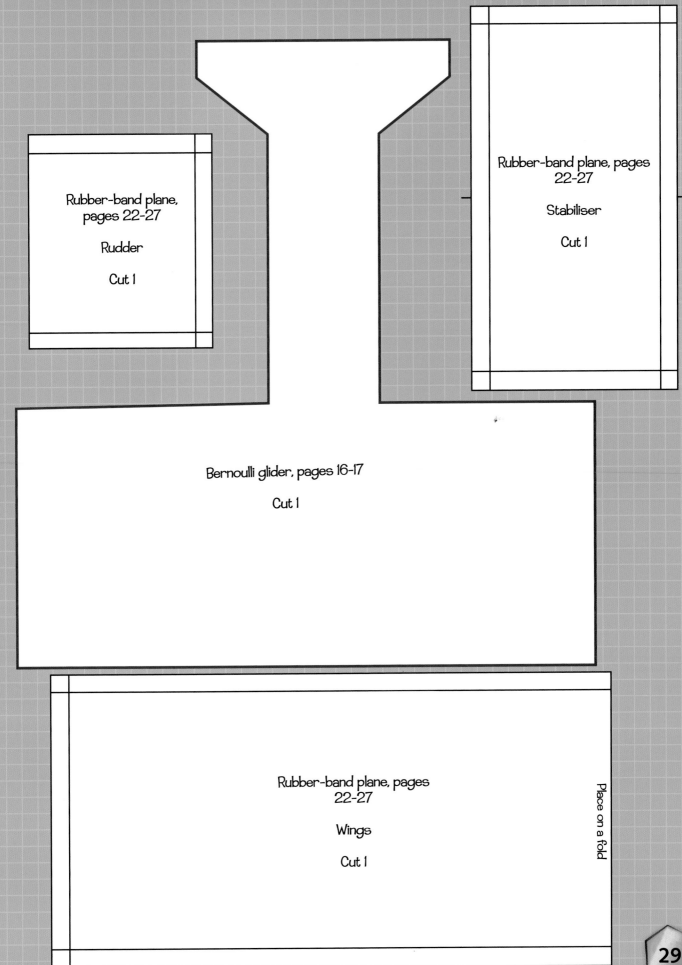

Rubber-band plane, pages 22-27

Stabiliser

Cut 1

Rubber-band plane,
pages 22-27

Rudder

Cut 1

Bernoulli glider, pages 16-17

Cut 1

Rubber-band plane, pages
22-27

Wings

Cut 1

Place on a fold

Aircraft timeline

The Italian artist, Leonardo da Vinci, was fascinated by flight. In 1485 he made several drawings of flying machines, including winged devices and an ornithopter, a human-powered flying machine.

1485

The first hot-air balloon was invented by Joseph-Michel and Jacques-Étienne Montgolfier. The balloon was powered by hot air generated by a fire beneath the basket. The first flight rose 1,000 m into the air while the second flight carried a sheep, a duck and a rooster on a flight that lasted 8 minutes. The same year, Jean-François Pilâtre de Rozier and François Laurent were the first passengers but this time the balloon was tethered to the ground.

1783

Sir George Cayley was an English engineer who was very influential in the history of aeronautics. Sometimes known as the *'father of aviation'*, he identified the four forces that act on an aeroplane in flight – lift, drag, thrust and gravity (see page 8). He recognised that an aeroplane would need power to keep it in the air for any length of time. In 1853, his coachman, John Appleby, made the first manned glider flight in a glider designed by Cayley.

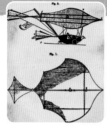

1853

1891-1896

Otto Lilienthal, a German engineer, designed the first glider capable of carrying a person and flying a long distance. His studied bird flight, conducted experiments and published his results in 1889. This book was used by the Wright brothers (see below left). His glider was similar to a modern hang-glider, with a bar to hang on to.

Alberto Santos-Dumont, a Brazilian aviator, won the Aero Club of France's prize in 1901. He successfully circled the Eiffel Tower and returned to his starting point in less than 30 minutes in the airship he'd designed.

1901

The first powered aeroplane flight occurred in 1903 at Kitty Hawk, North Carolina, USA. Orville and Wilbur Wright had been designing and testing gliders since 1899. In 1903 they added an engine to their best design and the *Flyer* made a 12-second flight on 17 December. By late 1905, their third powered aeroplane could make flights that lasted several minutes.

1903

1927

American aviator, Charles Lindbergh, completed the first solo, non-stop trans-Atlantic flight. He flew from New York, USA, to Paris, France.

1930

Frank Whittle, a British engineer and RAF pilot, patented the first jet engine in 1930. The first British jet aircraft with a Whittle engine flew in 1941.

1932

American aviator, Amelia Earhart, was the first woman to make a solo non-stop trans-Atlantic flight.

Concorde carried passengers on supersonic flights, cutting journey times in half. Concorde broke the sound barrier, causing noise pollution in the form of a sonic boom.

1976-2003

Now
We take air transport for granted to carry passengers, food stuffs and other goods as well as military equipment and troops.

Glossary

Aerodynamics The way that air moves around moving objects.

Airtight Not allowing air to pass through.

Aviator Someone who flies aircraft.

Catapult A machine that helps launch things into the air.

Drag A force that pulls back on a moving object.

Energy The ability to do work; it comes in several forms including heat, light, chemical energy and electricity.

Force A push or a pull.

Friction A force that slows down movement when one surface slides over another.

Glider A type of flying machine without an engine.

Gravity A force of attraction. Earth's gravity pulls everything towards the ground.

Lift The upward force produced on a wing when it moves through the air.

Patent A licence granting the sole right for a set period of time to make, use or sell an invention.

Sonic boom A loud noise that occurs when an object travels faster than the speed of sound – called breaking the sound barrier.

Thrust A pushing force that moves something forward.

Further information

Design a plane of the future:

www.nasa.gov/audience/forstudents/5-8/features/F_Design_Plane_of_Future.html

Build the world record-holding paper plane:
www.aviation-for-kids.com/paper-airplanes.html

Escape the jungle by building your own plane:
www.nms.ac.uk/explore/play/plane-builder/

Design a real plane:
www.juniorflyer.com/posts/design-your-own-aircraft/

Index

Crafts and parts suppliers

Craft shops, art shops, office suppliers and stationery shops will sell most of the materials you will need to build the models in this book – and you will be able to use materials you have at home or at school.

A good online craft store is: www.bakerross.co.uk

This electronics supplier sells electric motors and other related components: www.maplin.co.uk

Rocket motors are available online from online suppliers including:
http://www.rapidonline.com
http://hurricanemodels.co.uk

Note to parents and teachers: every effort has been made by the Publishers to ensure that these websites are suitable for children, that they are of the highest educational value, and that they contain no inappropriate or offensive material. However, because of the nature of the Internet, it is impossible to guarantee that the contents of these sites will not be altered. We strongly advise that Internet access is supervised by a responsible adult.